© 2025 Six Crown Publishing™
All rights reserved. No part of this publication may be reproduced, distributed, or transmitted in any form or by any means, including photocopying, recording, or other electronic or mechanical methods, without the prior written permission of the publisher, except in the case of brief quotations embodied in critical reviews and certain other noncommercial uses permitted by copyright law.

The Alchemy Crown™: A Guide to Confidence, Clarity & Self-Discovery - Teen Edition
by Victoria B. Wright
First Edition
ISBN: 979-8-9997687-5-9
Printed in the United States of America

Hey you.

Yeah, you — the one holding this book like it might spill secrets.

Life as a teen is a whole movie — plot twists, new chapters, and a soundtrack that changes with every mood. Some days you're the main character, other days the background extra.

This book is your pocket-sized hype squad and reality check in one.

Flip to a page. Take the message how you need it.

Some messages will hype you up, some will make you think, and some will make you laugh — all here to remind you that your story is just getting good.

— Victoria B. Wright

Your worth isn't measured in followers.

(Social Media & Comparison)

A good attitude can get you further than a perfect score.

(School & Ambition)

Find your "why."

(Independence & Self-Discovery)

You're allowed to step back for your mental health.

(Family)

Stay curious.

(School & Ambition)

Being single is better than being half-loved.

(Love & Crushes)

If they like you, you'll know.
If they don't, you'll be confused.

(Love & Crushes)

Try new things without fear of failure.

(Independence & Self-Discovery)

You can change your mind about your future.

(Independence & Self-Discovery)

Rest is productive too.

(Mental Health)

Eat the fries — always eat the fries.

(Just for Fun)

Love your people, but take care of yourself first.

(Family)

Your worth isn't measured in likes.

(Confidence & Self-Esteem)

You can learn from your family's past and create your own path.

(Family)

Forgiveness is for your peace, not their comfort.

(Family)

Real friends clap for you when you win.

(Friendships)

Be curious, not afraid.

(Independence & Self-Discovery)

Loyalty is a two-way street.

(Friendships)

Your standards aren't too high —
they're just yours.

(Love & Crushes)

Never shrink to make others comfortable.

(Confidence & Self-Esteem)

Wear mismatched socks proudly.

(Just for Fun)

Some people are lessons, others are blessings.

(Life Lessons)

Sometimes the friends you choose can feel like family, too.

(Family)

Tradition an be beautiful – but so can new ideas.

(Family)

Apologize when you're wrong —
it's strength, not weakness.

(Life Lessons)

It's okay to say "I need help."

(Mental Health)

Your circle should want to see you win.

(Friendships)

Change is scary, but so is staying stuck.

(Life Lessons)

Wear the outfit just because.

(Life Lessons)

Sometimes the sibling you fight with becomes your best friend later.

(Family)

Celebrate small wins.

(Mental Health)

Don't dim your sparkle for anyone.

(Confidence & Self-Esteem)

Healing isn't linear.

(Mental Health)

Don't beg for someone's attention.

(Love & Crushes)

Boundaries are love in action.

(Family)

Your real ones will stay through the plot twists.

(Friendships)

Curate your feed for positivity.

(Social Media & Comparison)

Likes don't define you —
they refresh and disappear.

(Social Media & Comparison)

You can forgive and still walk away.

(Life Lessons)

You're the main character. Act like it.

(Confidence & Self-Esteem)

Don't lose yourself trying to keep someone.

(Love & Crushes)

The best friendships survive awkward silences.

(Friendships)

Your voice matters.

(Independence & Self-Discovery)

Ask questions — it's how you get answers.

(School & Ambition)

Never stop learning.

(School & Ambition)

Watch the sunset without your phone.

(Just for Fun)

You can be kind without being a doormat.

(Life Lessons)

Not everyone will like you — and that's okay.

(Life Lessons)

Be your own biggest supporter.

(Independence & Self-Discovery)

Not everyone is meant to sit at
your lunch table forever.

(Friendships)

A healthy crush shouldn't hurt your self-esteem.

(Love & Crushes)

Post what makes you happy.

(Social Media & Comparison)

Jealousy has no place in real friendship.

(Friendships)

Protect your peace, even if it
means eating alone sometimes.

(Friendships)

If they don't respect you, it's not love.

(Love & Crushes)

Don't compete with your friends — cheer for them.

(Friendships)

Family support can be quiet but still powerful.

(Family)

Your dreams are valid, no matter how big.

(Independence & Self-Discovery)

Your mental health is worth prioritizing.

(Mental Health)

You don't need to explain your growth.

(Independence & Self-Discovery)

Don't fear being underestimated —
surprise them.

(Independence & Self-Discovery)

Bake cookies at midnight.

(Just for Fun)

Learn to enjoy your own company.

(Life Lessons)

Glow from the inside first.

(Confidence & Self-Esteem)

Not every crush is meant to be a relationship.

(Love & Crushes)

You don't have to explain why you need space.

(Mental Health)

Your dreams are valid, even if
not everyone understands them yet.

(Family)

Try a hairstyle you've never done before.

(Just for Fun)

Breathe — it's free therapy.

(Mental Health)

Keep your head high and your standards higher.

(Confidence & Self-Esteem)

You're the author of your own future story.

(Family)

It's okay to take care of your well-being while staying connected to family.

(Family)

You can't force someone to treat you right.

(Friendships)

Write a letter to your future self.

(Just for Fun)

Laugh at your own jokes.

(Just for Fun)

It's okay if you can't do it all today.

(Mental Health)

Life's too short to pretend you don't care.

(Life Lessons)

Outgrowing people is normal.

(Friendships)

Asking for help is brave.

(Mental Health)

Not every opinion deserves a reply.

(Social Media & Comparison)

You're allowed to stand alone.

(Independence & Self-Discovery)

Make choices for you, not for approval.

(Independence & Self-Discovery)

Protect your energy online.

(Social Media & Comparison)

Effort is the real flex.

(School & Ambition)

Even small progress counts.

(School & Ambition)

Never chase someone who isn't chasing you.

(Love & Crushes)

Take a random day to do nothing.

(Just for Fun)

Don't believe everything you see.

(Social Media & Comparison)

Every day is a chance to try again.

(Life Lessons)

You can start over anytime.

(Independence & Self-Discovery)

Study smart, not just hard.

(School & Ambition)

Don't confuse chemistry with compatibility.

(Love & Crushes)

Hard work now pays off later — trust the process.

(School & Ambition)

Not everyone will understand your path — walk it anyway.

(Independence & Self-Discovery)

Learn the lesson, not just the material.

(School & Ambition)

Take pride in your work.

(School & Ambition)

The right people don't make
you question your worth.

(Friendships)

You are not your mistakes.

(Mental Health)

Growth feels uncomfortable for a reason.

(Life Lessons)

Saying "no" is a full sentence.

(Life Lessons)

Stargaze and make a wish.

(Just for Fun)

Being yourself is your biggest flex.

(Confidence & Self-Esteem)

It's okay to outgrow people, places,
and versions of yourself.

(Independence & Self-Discovery)

Your future self will thank you for studying just one more hour.

(School & Ambition)

Your mistakes don't define you.

(Confidence & Self-Esteem)

Don't cheat yourself by slacking.

(School & Ambition)

Friends who hype you up are keepers.

(Friendships)

Social media should be fun, not stressful.

(Social Media & Comparison)

You don't need permission to dream big.

(Independence & Self-Discovery)

Take notes like you're writing a bestseller.

(School & Ambition)

It's okay to be different from your family.

(Family)

Someone who wants you will make time for you.

(Love & Crushes)

Your feelings are valid —
even if no one else understands.

(Mental Health)

It's okay to cry.

(Mental Health)

Take breaks from scrolling.

(Social Media & Comparison)

Respect is strongest when it's shared
by everyone in the family.

(Family)

Protect your mind like you protect your phone —
keep it safe from junk.

(Mental Health)

Learn skills you'll need for life.

(Independence & Self-Discovery)

Treat yourself to dessert first.

(Just for Fun)

Not all "influencers" are worth following.

(Social Media & Comparison)

You're proof that "one of one" exists.

(Confidence & Self-Esteem)

Mistakes mean you're trying.

(Life Lessons)

Your voice matters, even if it shakes.

(Confidence & Self-Esteem)

Silence can be an answer too.

(Life Lessons)

You can wish someone well and still walk away.

(Friendships)

You don't have to have it all figured out at 16.

(Mental Health)

You're not "too much" —
they're just not enough.

(Confidence & Self-Esteem)

A true friend will check you with love.

(Friendships)

The right friends bring out the best in you.

(Friendships)

Mixed signals are a signal — move on.

(Love & Crushes)

Try a hobby with zero pressure to be good.

(Just for Fun)

Take a scenic walk and leave your phone behind.

(Just for Fun)

Take your time — love isn't a race.

(Love & Crushes)

Explore what makes you happy.

(Independence & Self-Discovery)

You can be happy and still need rest.

(Mental Health)

You're allowed to log off.

(Mental Health)

Not everything needs to be posted.

(Social Media & Comparison)

The best outfit is your self-belief.

(Confidence & Self-Esteem)

Say yes to an adventure.

(Just for Fun)

You don't have to be perfect to be successful.

(School & Ambition)

Laugh so hard your stomach hurts.

(Just for Fun)

Protect your wins from the wrong ears.

(Friendships)

Stand for something or you'll fall for anything.

(Independence & Self-Discovery)

Family should be a place where
you feel safe and supported.

(Family)

Never stop asking "why?"

(Life Lessons)

Start a silly tradition with friends.

(Just for Fun)

You are not a burden.

(Mental Health)

Walk in like you own the place —
even if it's just math class.

(Confidence & Self-Esteem)

Your value doesn't decrease if they can't see it.

(Love & Crushes)

You're not behind,
you're just on your own timeline.

(Confidence & Self-Esteem)

Procrastination steals from your future self.

(School & Ambition)

Dance like nobody's screenshotting.

(Just for Fun)

Protect your peace at all costs.

(Life Lessons)

Being different is a gift.

(Independence & Self-Discovery)

It's okay to ask for help.

(School & Ambition)

Stand tall — your crown is showing.

(Confidence & Self-Esteem)

Some family bonds grow with time,
others fade — both are okay.

(Family)

You're allowed to take up space.

(Confidence & Self-Esteem)

Be the kind of person you'd look up to.

(Confidence & Self-Esteem)

Don't ignore the signs of burnout.

(Mental Health)

Build habits you'll thank yourself for.

(School & Ambition)

Good friends tell you when you have spinach in your teeth.

(Friendships)

Try a new food just to say you did.

(Just for Fun)

You're not behind just because
someone else is ahead.

(Social Media & Comparison)

You're allowed to rewrite your story.

(Life Lessons)

Show up prepared — it's half the battle.

(School & Ambition)

Love yourself first.

(Love & Crushes)

Don't let one bad grade rewrite your story.

(School & Ambition)

The world doesn't revolve around you —
but your life does.

(Life Lessons)

Take silly pictures with your friends.

(Just for Fun)

Don't compare your day one
to someone else's year five.

(Social Media & Comparison)

You're capable of more than you think.

(School & Ambition)

Mute what messes with your peace.

(Social Media & Comparison)

Protect your heart like it's your phone —
with a password.

(Love & Crushes)

School is temporary — knowledge lasts forever.

(School & Ambition)

Your vibe introduces you before you say a word.

(Confidence & Self-Esteem)

The right person won't make you
question if you're enough.

(Love & Crushes)

Popular doesn't always mean happy.

(Friendships)

Take responsibility for your actions,
not for everyone else's.

(Life Lessons)

Saying "I'm not okay" is
a step toward being okay.

(Mental Health)

No one has it together all the time.

(Mental Health)

You're allowed to start over —
as many times as you need.

(Confidence & Self-Esteem)

Fake friends will expose themselves — let them.

(Friendships)

Your laugh is your superpower.

(Confidence & Self-Esteem)

It's okay to hope for and work toward a better future.

(Family)

Learn skills, not just facts.

(School & Ambition)

Some people are just lessons in disguise.

(Friendships)

Small steps still count as progress.

(Mental Health)

Your mental health matters as much as your physical health.

(Mental Health)

People show you who they are —
believe them.

(Mental Health)

You can care about someone and
still set healthy boundaries.

(Family)

Say yes to experiences that excite you.

(Independence & Self-Discovery)

The mirror can't reflect everything amazing about you.

(Confidence & Self-Esteem)

Take risks that help you grow.

(Independence & Self-Discovery)

People can fake anything on the internet.

(Social Media & Comparison)

Your story is worth telling.

(Confidence & Self-Esteem)

You're not "lucky," you're deserving.

(Confidence & Self-Esteem)

Make friendship bracelets.

(Just for Fun)

Grades matter, but your mental health matters more.

(School & Ambition)

Teachers remember the respectful ones.

(School & Ambition)

Sing like you're on stage.

(Just for Fun)

You don't owe anyone access to you.

(Friendships)

Celebrate yourself for no reason at all.

(Just for Fun)

Being family doesn't always mean you'll be best friends — and that's okay.

(Family)

Choose progress over perfection.

(Life Lessons)

Choose peace over pressure.

(Mental Health)

You can love people from a distance.

(Friendships)

Private life = peaceful life.

(Social Media & Comparison)

Don't let the algorithm control your mood.

(Social Media & Comparison)

You can set boundaries with relatives too.

(Family)

Likes fade, character lasts.

(Social Media & Comparison)

Never trade your authenticity for approval.

(Life Lessons)

Jealousy isn't cute — it's toxic.

(Love & Crushes)

Learn from every season of your life.

(Independence & Self-Discovery)

Remember, unfollowing is self-care.

(Social Media & Comparison)

Friendships should be safe spaces.

(Friendships)

You can't pour from an empty cup.

(Life Lessons)

Don't chase clout — chase purpose.

(Social Media & Comparison)

Boundaries are self-care.

(Mental Health)

If they ghost you, let them stay gone.

(Love & Crushes)

One test won't define your intelligence.

(School & Ambition)

Spend time figuring out who you are.

(Independence & Self-Discovery)

Stop waiting for permission to shine.

(Confidence & Self-Esteem)

Some doors close so better ones can open.

(Life Lessons)

Trust your gut — it's usually right.

(Life Lessons)

Build the life you want,
not the one others expect.

(Independence & Self-Discovery)

You're not hard to love, they're just not ready.

(Love & Crushes)

Don't ignore red flags just
because you're comfortable.

(Friendships)

Love should make you feel safe.

(Love & Crushes)

The right choice isn't always the easy one.

(Life Lessons)

Therapy is for everyone.

(Mental Health)

People post their highlights, not their bloopers..

(Social Media & Comparison)

It's okay to support your family
without carrying all the weight.

(Family)

You don't owe strangers an explanation.

(Social Media & Comparison)

Don't settle for crumbs when
you deserve the whole cake.

(Love & Crushes)

Someone who truly likes you will show it.

(Love & Crushes)

Some friendships are for a season, not a lifetime.

(Friendships)

The internet isn't your diary.

(Social Media & Comparison)

You can't control everything,
but you can control your playlist.

(Life Lessons)

Filters aren't the truth.

(Social Media & Comparison)

Even your awkward phase is iconic.

(Confidence & Self-Esteem)

Education is power.

(School & Ambition)

Take breaks before you burn out.

(Mental Health)

Give yourself grace.

(Mental Health)

Your potential is limitless.

(School & Ambition)

Don't rush your journey.

(Life Lessons)

Limit your doomscrolling.

(Social Media & Comparison)

Don't fall for potential — fall for reality.

(Love & Crushes)

Your dreams deserve a solid plan.

(School & Ambition)

You can be strong and still struggle.

(Mental Health)

Listen to your body and mind.

(Mental Health)

Trust the timing of your life.

(Independence & Self-Discovery)

It's okay to love family while
keeping healthy space.

(Family)

Trust yourself.

(Independence & Self-Discovery)

Bad days don't mean a bad life.

(Mental Health)

Comparison kills joy.

(Social Media & Comparison)

Smile like you know a secret.

(Confidence & Self-Esteem)

Learn to enjoy your own company.

(Independence & Self-Discovery)

Your hustle will open doors.

(School & Ambition)

Even in family, kindness and
respect go both ways.

(Family)

Organization is a superpower.

(School & Ambition)

You don't need to fit in to stand out.

(Confidence & Self-Esteem)

Friends should make you feel lighter,
not drained.

(Friendships)

Distance doesn't ruin real friendships.

(Friendships)

Social media is not real life.

(Social Media & Comparison)

The glow-up is coming — be patient.

(Confidence & Self-Esteem)

Build a pillow fort.

(Just for Fun)

You're worth the wait.

(Love & Crushes)

You are your best investment.

(Independence & Self-Discovery)